EX LIBRIS

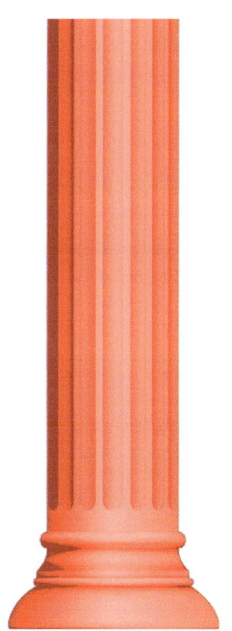

'Elegantly presented, entertaining, and educational.'
Ruth Downie, author.

'The perfect book for anyone who, like me, wishes they had understood Latin at school. Why did our teachers tell us it is a "dead language", and not how useful it would be in real life?'
Janie Hampton, author.

'A thoroughly helpful volume, great for both reference and pleasure, ideal for both the crossword and the classroom.'
Michelle Lovric, author.

Caroline K. Mackenzie read Classics at Pembroke College, Cambridge. After a legal career in London, she became Head of Classics at a school in Sevenoaks. In 2018 Caroline was awarded distinction in an MA in Classical Art and Archaeology at King's College London. Caroline offers online private tutoring in Latin and Greek and runs online Classical reading groups for all ages and abilities. Caroline's first book, *Culture and Society at Lullingstone Roman Villa* was published by Archaeopress in 2019.
Read more at www.carolinetutor.co.uk

A Latin Lexicon

An illustrated compendium of Latin words and English derivatives

Caroline K. Mackenzie

Archaeopress Publishing Ltd
Summertown Pavilion
18-24 Middle Way
Summertown
Oxford OX2 7LG

www.archaeopress.com

ISBN 978-1-78969-762-9
ISBN 978-1-78969-763-6 (e-Pdf)

Text: © Caroline K. Mackenzie 2020
Design and Layout: © Archaeopress 2020
Caroline K. Mackenzie asserts the moral right to be identified as the author of this work.

Cover image and illustrations in the text
© Amanda Short (Amanda Short Design)
www.amandashortdesign.com

All rights reserved. No part of this book may be reproduced, or transmitted, in any form or by any means, electronic, mechanical, photocopying or otherwise, without the prior written permission of the copyright owners.

This book is available direct from Archaeopress or from our website www.archaeopress.com

Acknowledgements

Thank you to Dr David Davison, Patrick Harris and Ben Heaney at Archaeopress for all their enthusiasm and advice. Particular thanks to Ben for his patience, zeal and hard work on the design of the book.

Immense thanks to Amanda Short for her fabulous and vibrant illustrations to accompany the Latin words, which she created with such detailed research and skill. Thank you also to Amanda for the beautiful cover image.

Thank you to Dr John Taylor for kindly reading a draft of the book and for his very helpful comments and suggestions. Any errors in the book are entirely my own. John was an ally and a muse when I embarked on my new career as a Classics teacher and his first-class Greek and Latin textbooks are constant companions.

Thank you to all the following (in alphabetical order) for their encouragement, friendship and mentoring: Professor Paul Cartledge, Mr Gordon Davy, Dr Daisy Dunn, Caroline Lawrence, Mrs Ursula Lee, Dr John Pearce and Dr John Taylor. Thank you also to all the History Girls, especially Ruth Downie, Janie Hampton, Mary Hoffman, Michelle Lovric and Celia Rees. For all her support and everything that she taught me during my legal career, thank you to Philippa Blake-Roberts.

My love of Latin all began thanks to a kind and inspirational Classics teacher at school, Mrs Jo Ruscoe. Her enthusiasm for both Latin and Greek was infectious and sparked a lifelong love of both languages.

Special mention is due to my Classics Club, especially those who have joined me for our online weekly Homer reading group during lockdown (when much of this book was written). They are an endless source of friendship, humour and motivation: Annie, Barbara, Barbarann, Beth, Christopher, Edward, Fiona, Frank, Gwen, Helga, Jenny, John, Karen, Kevin, Miles, and Sophie. I have also very much enjoyed studying Homeric Greek with Allan Nichols.

For their lifelong (and transatlantic) love and support and for being such positive influences, huge personal thanks to Professor Mike and Mrs Penny Buckingham.

Most important of all, my heartfelt thanks to all my family. Special thanks to my lovely sister and nephew, Liz and Tom Dargie, for always being there and for bringing me endless supplies of books and chocolate. Thank you to my wonderful parents for absolutely everything, especially all their love and guidance. I miss Dad hugely but am so grateful for the time we all had with him and his devotion to the family. Dad was always kind, gentle and giving, and had a great sense of humour. Mum - you are amazing and continue to inspire me every day; thank you for all our coffees, chats and walks in the countryside. Grannie would be so proud of you. Thank you in turn to Grannie for being such an inspiration - full of kindness and just a little bit of mischief. Finally, and forever, thank you to my wonderful husband, Jock, for being my twenty-four-hour IT helpdesk, my soul mate, and for being by my side (in every sense) during our odyssey through life.

Preface

The idea for this book arose from many happy hours spent with my pupils who were striving to learn their Latin vocabulary. Together we devised a game where we would think of an English derivative from a Latin word, which would then provide a clue to the meaning of the Latin; e.g. *rideo* means 'I laugh' or 'I smile', and some English derivatives are 'deride' or 'ridiculous'. We soon discovered that the Latin words were easy to recall and learning became much more efficient as well as fun.

Around this time, I used to hear commuters on the train mumbling to themselves as they sought the answers to their daily crossword. Often, I realised that Latin words were behind both the clues and the answers. It seemed the above technique of associating derivatives with their Latin origin might help with word puzzles and similar activities, too.

The purpose of this book is threefold. First, all the words I have chosen (with just two exceptions) are required for the Oxford Cambridge and RSA ('the OCR') GCSE syllabus and therefore this book can be used as a revision aid for GCSE students. For this reason, I have included some grammatical information for each word, such as the declension and gender of a noun and the conjugation of a verb. Secondly, the book is intended as a secret weapon for anyone tackling crosswords or word games, where the associations between Latin vocabulary and the English derivatives will spark the imagination and encourage a deluge of possible answers. Last and certainly not least, the overriding aim of this book is to provide enjoyment. I hope you will find it fun, challenging and a fitting celebration of the magnificent Latin language.

For all my pupils, past and present.

Introduction

Notes for GCSE students

There are 450 prescribed words on the OCR GCSE Defined Vocabulary List ('the OCR List') and 360 of them are included in this book. I have also included 10 irregular comparative and superlative forms of adjectives which you need to know, and all the prescribed cardinal numbers (1 to 10, 100 and 1,000). I have included just two words which do not appear on the OCR List ('ante' and 'soror' for the reasons given in the footnotes to those entries). If you learn all the vocabulary by heart, you will be able to tackle translations and comprehensions with confidence and flair. Words in the vocabulary list are quite simply the building blocks that you need to achieve a solid standing in Latin. Combined with a firm grasp of the grammar, knowledge of the vocabulary really is the key to success.

As a guide to the grammar, I strongly recommend John Taylor's *Essential GCSE Latin* (Third Edition, Bloomsbury, 2017) which sets out the rules succinctly and includes excellent practice passages.

Nouns

Nouns are shown in the nominative singular then the genitive singular. The genitive provides the stem. The gender is also given: masculine (masc.), feminine (fem.) or neuter (neut.). Underneath each noun, the declension (or group) to which that noun belongs is shown as 1st, 2nd, 3rd, 4th or 5th. The numbers are presented in this way to distinguish them from the numbers of conjugations (shown as first, second, etc.) which apply to the verbs.

Adjectives

Adjectives are shown in the following order: masculine, feminine, then neuter. If the feminine is the same as the masculine, it is not repeated so the two forms shown are: masculine/feminine, then neuter. Some 3rd declension adjectives are given instead with the genitive singular as this provides the stem, e.g. 'felix, (gen.) felicis'.[1]

---

[1] On these types of adjectives see Taylor p. 26.

Verbs

Verbs are shown with their principal parts, which give the following information: present tense (first person singular), present infinitive (which indicates to which conjugation the verb belongs), perfect tense (first person singular) and, where applicable, perfect passive participle. The fourth principal part of a verb is often the best place to start when trying to guess a derivative from that verb.

Verbs belong to different conjugations, or families, which determine how they are formed. The conjugations are shown beneath the principal parts as first, second, third or fourth. The numbers are presented in this way to distinguish them from the numbers of declensions (shown as 1st, 2nd, etc.) which apply to the nouns. Some verbs are 'mixed' conjugations and are shown as third/fourth. These verbs are treated as third conjugation because their infinitive ends in -*ere* but their present, imperfect and future tenses are the same as the fourth conjugation.[2]

Deponent verbs are marked as such. These are verbs which are passive in form but active in meaning. There are also three semi-deponent verbs.[3]

Adverbs

The adverbs included are indeclinable which means they do not change their endings.

Cases

A case, such as the ablative or dative, is used for a noun, pronoun or adjective to show the role it is playing in the sentence. The prepositions included in this book are shown with the case by which they are usually followed, e.g. 'ad (+ accusative)' (to, towards) and it is worth learning both parts together. Most verbs are followed by an accusative and this is the default unless the entry states otherwise. However, some verbs use the dative, e.g. 'credo' (I trust) (literally, 'I give my trust *to* you'). These verbs are shown as taking the dative as, again, it is worth learning this at the same time as the meaning of the verb.

---

[2] On mixed conjugations see Taylor p. 68.
[3] On deponent and semi-deponent verbs see Taylor pp. 99–101.

The names of the different cases are themselves Latin derivatives and these may help explain the purpose of each case:

'nominative' from 'nomen' (name) Subject
It 'names' the subject of a sentence or clause.

'vocative' from 'voco' (I call) Addressing
Used for addressing or 'calling' someone.

'accusative' from 'accuso'[4] (I accuse) Object
It aims at or 'holds accountable' the object
of a sentence or clause.

'genitive' from 'gens' (family, people) Of
It denotes that something belongs to another,
or is 'of' another (as if of its 'family').

'dative' from 'do' (I give) ('do, dare, dedi, *datus*') To, for
Usually denotes giving: 'I give a gift *to* you' or,
'this gift is *for* you'.

'ablative' from 'a, ab' (from, by) and 'ablatus' From, by, with
(see 'aufero, auferre, abstuli, *ablatus*') (carry away)
Indicates 'away from', or simply 'from', 'by', or
sometimes 'with'.

'Irregular' words

Some Latin words (in this list, mainly verbs) do not belong to one of the standard conjugations or declensions. They are known as 'irregular' and are shown in the list as 'irreg.'

---

[4] 'accuso' is not on the OCR List. It means 'I accuse, blame, or find fault with' and the connection here seems to be that the accusative case 'aims at', 'focuses on' or 'holds accountable' the object of a sentence or clause.

General notes

Choice of derivatives

This is by no means an exhaustive list of all the possible derivatives. Many of the Latin words have numerous derivatives in English but I have limited the number of derivatives per word to a maximum of six, except where there is a cross-reference to another entry where one or two additional ones may be included. There is also space on each page for you to add some more derivatives if you wish to do so.

Cross-references are marked up 'cf.' followed by the relevant Latin word, being the first word in the respective entry. If the cross-reference applies to the whole entry, I have included it on a separate line from the derivatives. If the cross-reference applies to one or more specific derivatives, then I have included it immediately following that derivative (or those derivatives) and not on a separate line.

If a derivative can be used in the English language in both its singular and plural forms (e.g. 'curator' and 'curators') I have simply included one of these (usually the singular). However, where a derivative gives us, say, both a verb and a noun, or both an adjective and an adverb, I have often included both, despite their apparent similarity. This is not repetition for its own sake but to demonstrate how ubiquitous the derivatives are in our language. Also, some students may be familiar with one derivative but not the others and, from a didactic point of view, my aim is to facilitate the learning of the Latin word by association with an already familiar English word.

I have not attempted to explain or distinguish whether derivatives come from the Latin verb or noun as that is beyond the scope of this book. Sometimes a Latin noun and verb (e.g. 'imperator' and 'impero') give us derivatives (empire, imperious, etc.) that can usefully be associated with both the noun and verb for the purposes of learning vocabulary. If the number of derivatives allow, I have included different ones for, say, the noun and the verb and cross-referenced them.

Some derivatives may seem obvious, e.g. 'resist' from 'resisto' whereas others are more surprising, e.g. why does a 'tandem' bike derive from 'tandem' (at last)? If we translate 'tandem' as 'at length' this begins to make more sense when we think of a tandem bike (for two people) simply as a lengthened version of a one-person bike. 'Tandem' is often confused with 'tamen' (however) but by imagining a picture of a tandem bike (see page CVI) and knowing the pun in the meaning, the distinction between the two words can easily be made.

For consistency, words that can end in either '-ise' or '-ize' are shown throughout with the ending '-ise'.

The derivatives are listed in alphabetical order within each entry for ease of reference.

Latin words and phrases in common usage

Some words and phrases which we use in English are taken direct from the Latin, e.g. 'alter ego'. One could argue that these are not strictly 'derivatives', and that they are simply Latin. I have, however, included them where I believe they are in sufficiently common usage to be familiar to many, if not all, readers. They are shown in inverted commas, e.g. 'bona fide'. For their meanings, please see the Glossary.

Derivatives in other languages

Of course, there are many Latin derivatives in other European languages such as Italian and French. With a few exceptions, limitations of space have precluded me from including other languages but this can be a very useful way for students to learn their vocabulary and there is space on each page for such comparisons to be noted. A good knowledge of Latin can improve one's vocabulary not only in English but in many other modern languages.

'Double derivatives'

The number of cross-references ('double derivatives' if you will) is large and while I have included most of them, for reasons of space and not wishing to clutter the pages, I have left some of these for you to spot for yourself. For example, 'facio' (I make) appears in many compound verbs and their derivatives (in forms such as '-fact', '-fic' and '-fy'). Likewise, prefixes such as 'pro-' (in front of) and 're-' (…back) recur frequently.

Names

Names, e.g. Benedict (see 'bene' and 'dico'), can be identified as such since they are the only derivatives that are given with an initial capital letter. There are numerous brand names (clothing lines, food products, furniture shops, etc.) which make good use of Latin (and Greek) derivatives. For copyright reasons I have not included them in the book, but readers may naturally be reminded of some of these when studying the meanings of the Latin words and it can be a useful way for students to remember vocabulary.

'It's all Greek…'

Of course, many Latin words themselves derive from Ancient Greek, e.g. 'hora' from 'ὥρα' (transliterated 'hora') but I have not attempted to show these as the aim of this book is to connect the Latin words to English. Ancient Greek is a wonderful language and deserves a derivatives book of its own.

Genders

If a Latin noun has very similar masculine and feminine forms, e.g. 'deus' for god and 'dea' for goddess, I have simply included the masculine as the derivatives are usually the same.[5]

Months of the year

The original Roman calendar comprised a ten-month year. Of those ten months, September was the seventh month, October was the eighth, November was the ninth, and December was the tenth. This explains why these months' names derive from their respective numbers. The additional two months (which make up our twelve) also have a Roman association - July after the emperor Gaius Julius Caesar (who was born in that month) and August after his adopted son and heir, Augustus.

Themes

I have avoided including terms which are very specialist, e.g. legal phrases such as 'res ipsa loquitur' (the thing speaks for itself) although another legal term 'caveat emptor' (buyer beware) may be more familiar from its use in our conveyancing system and therefore is included. Musical terms such as 'cadence' from 'cado' (I fall) or 'alto' from 'altus' (high or deep) will be well-known to musicians but have only been included if I believe they may also be familiar to other readers, too. Even the world of information technology embraces Latin derivatives such as 'cursor' from 'curro' (I run) and 'delete' from 'deleo' (I destroy). While 'dormy' from 'dormio' (I sleep) is probably only known to golfers and was a new discovery for me, I could not resist including it.[6]

---

[5] 'rex' (king) and 'regina' (queen) have both been included as these are not as easy to deduce from each other.
[6] It means a player is as many holes ahead as there are still to play so (s)he cannot lose even if (s)he goes to sleep.

Other themes that I frequently encountered in my research (perhaps unsurprisingly) were those of flowers ('gladiolus') and nature ('brevipennate'), the church ('Advent' and 'laetare'), medicine and anatomy ('vertebra'), vocations ('horologist'), sport ('equestrian') and theatre (stage directions given in Latin such as 'loquitor', 'exeunt', etc.). You may wish to use this book as the starting point for collecting further derivatives within a theme of your choice.

Derivatives in grammar

Even the word 'derivative' is itself a derivative, being literally something flowing downstream (the verb 'derivare' means to turn into another channel or to divert from). Likewise, 'declension' derives from 'declinare' (to bend away from), 'conjugation' from 'coniugare' (to join together or to connect) and 'language' from 'lingua' (tongue). Many other grammatical terms appear throughout the derivatives given in this book as summarised below. (For the derivation of the names of cases, see 'Cases' above.)

'active' from 'ago' (I do, act)

'adjective' from 'ad' (to, towards) and 'iacio' (I throw)

'adverb' from 'ad' (to, towards) and 'verbum' (word)

'case' from 'cado' (I fall)

'dictionary' from 'dico' (I say)

'feminine' from 'femina' (woman)

'noun' from 'nomen' (name)

'object' from 'iacio' (I throw)

'passive' from 'patior' (I suffer, endure)

'preposition' from 'pono' (I place, put)

'sentence' from 'sentio' (I feel)

'subject' from 'sub' (under) and 'iacio' (I throw)

'tense' from 'tempus' (time)

'verb' from 'verbum' (word)

'vocabulary' from 'voco' (I call)

Further reading

For more detailed etymology and the meanings of any of the words in this book, see *The Chambers Dictionary* (Revised Thirteenth Edition, Chambers Harrap Publishers Ltd., 2016).

John Taylor's *Essential GCSE Latin* (Third Edition, Bloomsbury, 2017).

For details of the specifications for the OCR (Oxford Cambridge and RSA) examination board's qualification in GCSE Latin, including the full Defined Vocabulary List, see OCR's website: https://www.ocr.org.uk

Latin phrases and their abbreviations

It would be remiss not to showcase throughout this book some of the common Latin phrases and their abbreviations that we use. For completeness, I set them out here with a literal translation for each. (They also appear in the Glossary.)

cf. 'confer' (compare)

e.g. 'exempli gratia' (for the sake of example)

etc. 'et cetera' (and the others)

N.B. 'nota bene' (note well)

vide (see)

Other abbreviations used in this book

fem. feminine

gen. genitive

irreg. irregular

masc. masculine

neut. neuter

pl. plural

Glossary:
Latin words and phrases in common usage

adsum	I am present; here
alma mater	one's former university, school or college (literally, 'nourishing mother')
alter ego	one's second self
anno domini or **A.D.**	in the year of our lord
ante meridiem or **a.m.**	before midday; morning
bona fide	genuine; in good faith
carpe diem	seize the day
caveat emptor	let the buyer beware; it is the buyer's responsibility
ceteris paribus or **cet. par.**	other things being equal
confer or **cf.**	compare
curriculum vitae or **C.V.**	a summary of one's life, especially details of education and career (literally, 'the course of life')
et alia or **et al.**	and other things
et cetera or **etc.**	and the rest; and so on

exeat	*formal leave of absence (literally, 'let him or her go out')*
exempli gratia or *e.g.*	*for (the sake of) example*
homo sapiens	*the human species (literally, 'wise human')*
ibidem or *ib.* or *ibid.*	*in the same place (used when referring to a book, article, etc. already cited)*
idem or *id.*	*the same; as mentioned before*
id est or *i.e.*	*that is*
inter alia	*among other things*
inter nos	*between ourselves*
ipso facto	*by that very fact*
mea culpa	*(by) my fault*
modus operandi	*a way of working; mode of operation*
nota bene or *N. B.*	*note well; take note*
per annum or *p.a.*	*each year*
per capita	*counting by heads; for each person*
per centum or *per cent.*	*for each hundred; percentage*

post meridiem or **p.m.**	after midday; afternoon
post scriptum or **P.S.**	an addition to the completed text of a book; introduces addition to a letter or other message (literally, 'written after')
prima facie	on first appearance; at first sight
pro rata	in proportion
pros and cons	advantages and disadvantages (from 'pro' and 'contra' so literally, 'for and against')
pro tempore or **pro tem.**	for the time being
quidnunc	an inquisitive, gossiping person (literally, 'what now?')
quid pro quo	something given or taken as equivalent to another (literally, 'something for something')
quod erat demonstrandum or **Q.E.D.**	which was to be demonstrated or proved
quod vide or **q.v.**	which see
re	concerning; with reference to (literally, '[in] the matter')
semper fidelis	always faithful
semper idem	always the same
semper paratus	always ready

sic	so; thus (often shown within brackets in quoted text to indicate that the original source is being strictly reproduced even though it may be incorrect)
sic passim	so throughout (used to show that a spelling, word, etc. has appeared in the same form throughout in a book, article, etc.)
sine die	without a day (appointed)
sine dubio	without doubt
sine qua non	a fundamental condition (literally, 'without which not…')
status quo	unchanged situation (literally, 'the state in which')
stet	an instruction to restore something which has been deleted (literally, 'let it stand')
summa cum laude	with greatest distinction (an academic award)
terra firma	the mainland; on solid ground
vade-mecum	a useful handbook that one carries with oneself for constant reference; a pocket companion (literally, 'go with me')
vice versa	the other way around (literally, 'the position having been turned')
vide	see
viva voce or *viva*	an oral academic examination (literally, 'with the living voice')

Latin Lexicon

A–V

A

a, ab (+ ablative)
(also used as a prefix with verbs)
preposition
from, away from, by
(as a prefix = away)
abnormal, abscond, abstain (cf. 'teneo')

absum, abesse, afui
verb *(irreg.)*
be absent, be away, be distant from
absence, absent, absentee, absenteeism, absently

accido, accidere, accidi
verb *(third)*
happen
accidence, accident, accidental, accidentally, accidented

A Latin Lexicon

accipio, accipere, accepi, acceptus

verb *(third/fourth)*

accept, take in, receive

accept, acceptability, acceptable, acceptance, accepted

ad (+ accusative)

(also used as a prefix with verbs)

preposition

to, towards, at

adapt, address, adhere, adhesion, adjective (cf. 'iacio'), advance, adverb (cf. 'verbum')

adsum, adesse, adfui

verb *(irreg.)*

be here, be present

'adsum', adessive

advenio, advenire, adveni

verb *(fourth)*

arrive

advent, adventure, adventuresome, adventurous

A

aedifico

aedifico, aedificare, aedificavi, aedificatus

verb *(first)*

build

edification, edifice, edificial, edify, edifying

ager, agri (masc.)

noun (2nd)

field

agrichemical, agricultural, agriculture, agrobiology, agroecosystem

ago, agere, egi, actus

verb *(third)*

do, act, drive

act, acting, action, active, actor, actressy, proactive (cf. 'pro')

A Latin Lexicon

alius, alia, aliud
adjective/pronoun

other, another, else

alias, alibi, alien, alienate, 'et alia' or 'et al.', 'inter alia' (cf. 'inter')

alter, altera, alterum
adjective/pronoun

the other, another, one (of two), the second (of two)

alter, 'alter ego' (cf. 'ego'), altercate, alternate, alternative, altruistic

altus, alta, altum
adjective

high, deep

altitonant, altitude, altitudinal, alto

ambulo, ambulare, ambulavi
verb *(first)*

walk

amble, ambler, ambulance, ambulant, ambulatory, noctambulation, noctambulist (cf. 'nox')

A

amicus, amici (masc.)
noun (2nd)
friend
amicability, amicable, amicableness, amicably

amo, amare, amavi, amatus
verb *(first)*
love, like
Amanda, amiable, amorous
(cf. 'amor')

amor, amoris (masc.)
noun (3rd)
love
Amanda, amiable, amorous
(cf. 'amo')

ancilla, ancillae (fem.)
noun (1st)
slave-girl, slave-woman
ancillary

A Latin Lexicon

animus, animi (masc.)

noun (2nd)

mind, spirit, soul

animated, animatic, animation, animator, inanimate

annus, anni (masc.)

noun (2nd)

year

'anno domini' or 'A.D.' (cf. 'dominus'), annual, annualise, annually, annuitant, annuity, biennial, centennial (cf. 'centum'), novennial (cf. 'novem'), 'per annum' or 'p.a.' (cf. 'per')

ante (+ accusative)[1]

preposition

before, in front of

antecedent, antechamber, 'ante meridiem' or 'a.m.' (cf. 'dies'), anteprandial, 'raise/up the ante'

---

[1] ante is not on the OCR List but is included for completeness to accompany 'antea' as the OCR List includes both 'post' and 'postea'.

A

antea
adverb
before, previously
vide 'ante'

appropinquo, appropinquare, appropinquavi (+ dative)
verb *(first)*
approach, come near to
approprinquate, appropinquation, appropinque, appropinquity

aqua, aquae (fem.)
noun (1st)
water
aqua, aquabatics, aquamarine (cf. mare), aquanautics (cf. 'nauta'), aquaphobia, aquaplane, aquarium, aquatic, aqueduct (cf. 'duco')

arma, armorum (neut. pl.)
noun (2nd)
arms, weapons
armament, armature, armed, armoury, arms

A Latin Lexicon

ars, artis (fem.)
noun (3rd)

art, skill

art, artefact, artful, artificial (cf. 'facio'), artistic, artistry, arty-farty

ascendo, ascendere, ascendi, ascensus
verb *(third)*

climb

ascend, ascendance, ascendancy, ascendent, ascension, ascent

audax, (gen.) audacis
adjective

bold, daring

audacious, audaciously, audaciousness, audacity
(cf. 'audeo')

audeo, audere, ausus sum
verb *(second) (semi-deponent)*

dare

audacious, audaciously, audaciousness, audacity
(cf. 'audax')

A

audio, audire, audivi, auditus

verb *(fourth)*

hear, listen to

audible, audiogram, audiograph, audiology, audiometer, audio-visual (cf. 'video'), auditory

aufero, auferre, abstuli, ablatus

verb *(irreg.)*

take away, carry off, steal

ablate, ablation, ablatitious, ablatival, ablative

auxilium, auxilii (neut.)

noun (2nd)

help

auxiliar, auxiliary

B

bellum, belli (neut.)

noun (2ⁿᵈ)

war

*Bellatrix, belligerence, belligerency, belligerent, belligerently
(cf. 'gero')*

bellum

B

bene

adverb

well

Benedict (cf. 'dico'), benefaction, benefactor, beneficial, beneficiary, benefit (cf. 'facio'), benevolent (cf. 'volo'), 'nota bene' or 'N.B.', omnibenevolent (cf. 'omnis')

bibo, bibere, bibi

verb *(third)*

drink

bib, bibacious, bibation, bibber, imbibe, imbibition

bonus, bona, bonum

adjective

good

'bona fide', bonus

brevis, breve

adjective

short, brief

abbreviate, abbreviation, brevipennate, brevity, briefcase, briefs

C

cado, cadere, cecidi, casus

verb *(third)*

fall

cadence, cadenced, cadent, cadential, cadenza, case

caelum, caeli (neut.)

noun (2nd)

sky, heaven

celeste, celestial, celestially, celestite, coelostat

capio, capere, cepi, captus

verb *(third/fourth)*

take, catch, capture, make (a plan)

capsule, caption, capture, conception, contraception (cf. 'contra'), inception (cf. 'in')
(cf. 'captivus')

C

captivus, captivi (masc.)
noun (2nd)

captive, prisoner

captivate, captivation, captive, captivity, captor, capturer (cf. 'capio')

caput, capitis (neut.)
noun (3rd)

head

capital, capitalise, capitulate, captain, decapitate, 'per capita', triceps (cf. 'tres')

castra, castrorum (neut. pl.)
noun (2nd)

camp

castle; 'caster', 'cester' and 'chester' in names of places in Britain, e.g. Chester, Cirencester, Grantchester, Lancaster, Manchester, Winchester

celer, celeris, celere
adjective

quick, fast

accelerate, acceleration, accelerator, accelerometer, celerity

A Latin Lexicon

celo, celare, celavi, celatus
verb *(first)*

hide

conceal, concealable, concealer, concealment

cena, cenae (fem.)
noun (1st)

dinner, meal

cenacle

centum
number

100

centenary, centennial (cf. 'annus'), centimetre, centipede (cf. 'pes'), century, 'per centum' or 'per cent' (cf. 'per'), quatercentenary (cf. 'quattuor'), quincentenary (cf. 'quinque')

ceteri, ceterae, cetera
adjective/pronoun

the rest, the others

'ceteris paribus' or 'cet. par.', 'et cetera' or 'etc.'

C

cibus

cibus, cibi (masc.)

noun (2ⁿᵈ)

food

cibation

circum (+ accusative)

preposition

around

*circle, circuit, circumambulate (cf. 'ambulo'),
circumference (cf. 'fero'), circumnavigate (cf. 'navigo'),
circumvent (cf. 'venio'), circus*

A Latin Lexicon

civis, civis (masc. and fem.)
noun (3rd)
citizen
civic, civil, civilian, civilisation, civilised, civility

clamo, clamare, clamavi, clamatus
verb *(first)*
shout
clamorous, clamorously, clamourer, exclaim, exclamation
(cf. 'clamor')

clamor, clamoris (masc.)
noun (3rd)
shout, shouting, noise
clamorousness, clamour, exclamational, exclamative, exclamatory
(cf. 'clamo')

clarus, clara, clarum
adjective
famous, clear, distinguished, bright
Claire, Clara, Clare, clarify, clarinet, clarion, clarity

C

cogito, cogitare, cogitavi, cogitatus
verb *(first)*

think, consider

cogitate, cogitation, cogitative, incogitable

cognosco, cognoscere, cognovi, cognitus
verb *(third)*

get to know, find out

cognition, cognitive, cognosce, incognito, recognise, recognition

cogo, cogere, coegi, coactus
verb *(third)*

force, compel

coact, coaction, coactive

comes, comitis (masc. and fem.)
noun (3rd)

comrade, companion

comital, comitative, comitatus

A Latin Lexicon

conficio, conficere, confeci, confectus
verb *(third/fourth)*

finish; wear out, exhaust

confect, confection, confectionary, confectioner, confectionery

conor, conari, conatus sum
verb *(first) (deponent)*

try

conation, conative, conatus

consilium, consilii (neut.)
noun (2nd)

plan, idea, advice

consilience, consilient

conspicio, conspicere, conspexi, conspectus
verb *(third/fourth)*

catch sight of, notice

conspectus, conspicuity, conspicuous, conspicuously, conspicuousness, inconspicuous

C

constituo, constituere, constitui, constitutus
verb *(third)*
decide
constituency, constituent, constitute, constitution, constitutional, constitutively

consul, consulis (masc.)
noun (3rd)
consul
consul, consulage, consular, consulate, consulship

consumo, consumere, consumpsi, consumptus
verb *(third)*
eat
consumable, consume, consumer, consumerism, consumption

contra (+ accusative)
preposition
against
contraband, contraception (cf. 'capio'), contradict (cf. 'dico'), contraflow, contraindicate, contrary, contrast, contravene (cf. 'venio'), 'pros and cons' (cf. 'pro')

A Latin Lexicon

convenio, convenire, conveni, conventus

verb *(fourth)*

come together, gather, meet

convene, convenience, convenient, convenor, convent, convention, reconvene (cf. 're' and 'venio')

copiae, copiarum (fem. pl.)

noun (1st)

forces, troops

copious, copiously, copiousness

corpus, corporis (neut.)

noun (3rd)

body

corporal, corporate, corporation, incorporate, incorporation

cras

adverb

tomorrow

procrastinate, procrastination, procrastinative, procrastinator, procrastinatory

C

credo, credere, credidi, creditus (+ dative)
verb *(third)*

believe, trust, have faith in

credence, credentials, credibility, credible, incredible, incredulous

crudelis, crudele
adjective

cruel

cruel, cruelly, cruelness, cruelty

cum (+ ablative)
preposition

with

'summa cum laude' (cf. 'summus' and 'laudo'),
as a combining form, e.g. 'kitchen-cum-dining-room', 'vade-mecum'

cupio, cupere, cupivi, cupitus
verb *(third/fourth)*

want, desire

Cupid, Cupid's bow, cupidinous, cupidity

A Latin Lexicon

cura, curae (fem.)

noun (1st)

care, worry

curacy, curate, curator, curatorship, cure, incurable, pedicure (cf. 'pes'), sinecure (cf. 'sine')

curro, currere, cucurri, cursus

verb *(third)*

run

currency, current, cursive, cursively, cursor, cursory, recur (cf. 're')

custodio, custodire, custodivi, custoditus

verb *(fourth)*

guard

custode, custodial, custodian, custodianship, custodier, custody (cf. 'custos')

custos, custodis (masc. and fem.)

noun (3rd)

guard

custode, custodial, custodian, custodianship, custodier, custody (cf. 'custodio')

D

de (+ ablative)

preposition

from, down from; about

deactivate, derivative, descend, descendant (cf. 'descendo'), descent, deseed, desensitise

debeo, debere, debui, debitus

verb *(second)*

owe, ought, should, must

debenture, debit, debt, debtee, debtor, indebted

decem

number

ten

decagon, December, decennary (cf. 'annus'), decimal, decimate, decimetre

A Latin Lexicon

defendo, defendere, defendi, defensus
verb *(third)*
defend
defence, defenceless, defendant, defender, defensive, indefensible

deleo, delere, delevi, deletus
verb *(second)*
destroy
delete, deletion, deletive, deletory

descendo, descendere, descendi, descensus
verb *(third)*
go down, come down
descend, descendable, descending, descension, descent
(cf. 'de')

deus, dei (masc.)
noun (2nd)
god
deific, deification, deiform, deify, deity

D

dico, dicere, dixi, dictus
verb *(third)*

say, speak, tell

Benedict (cf. 'bene'), contradict (cf. 'contra'), dictate, dictation, diction, dictionary, dictum

dies, diei (masc. and fem.)
noun (5th)

day

'ante meridiem' or 'a.m.' (cf. 'ante'), 'carpe diem', diarise, diary, diurnal, 'post meridiem' or 'p.m.' (cf. 'post'), quotidian (cf. 'quot')

difficilis, difficile
adjective

difficult

difficult, difficulty

diligens, (gen.) diligentis
adjective

careful

diligence, diligent, diligently

A Latin Lexicon

dirus, dira, dirum
adjective

dreadful

dire, direful, direfully, direfulness, direness

discedo, discedere, discessi
verb *(third)*

depart, leave

decease, deceased

diu
adverb

for a long time

diuturnal, diuturnity

do, dare, dedi, datus
verb *(first)*

give

*data, dative, donate, donation, donee, donor
(cf. 'donum')*

D

doceo, docere, docui, doctus

verb *(second)*

teach

doctor, doctoral, doctorate, doctrine, document, documentary

dominus, domini (masc.)

noun (2ⁿᵈ)

master

'anno domini' or 'A.D.' (cf. 'annus'), dominant, dominate, domination, domineer, dominion, domino

domus, domus (fem.)

noun (4ᵗʰ)

home, house

domestic, domesticated, domesticity, domicile, domiciliary

donum, doni (neut.)

noun (2ⁿᵈ)

gift, present

donate, donation, donee, donor
(cf. 'do')

A Latin Lexicon

dormio

dormio, dormire, dormivi

verb *(fourth)*

sleep

dormant, dormer, dormitive, dormitory, dormouse, dormy

duco, ducere, duxi, ductus

verb *(third)*

lead, take

aqueduct (cf. 'aqua'), duct, ductile, ductility, viaduct (cf. 'via')
(cf. 'dux')

D

duo, duae, duo

number

two

dual, duathlon, duel, duet, duo

dux, ducis (masc.)

noun (3rd)

leader

duct, ducted, ductless, ductileness, ducting
(cf. 'duco')

E

e, ex (+ ablative)

(also used as a prefix with verbs)

preposition

from, out, out of

ex-, e.g. ex-boyfriend, ex-directory, ex-employer, etc., 'exeat' (cf. 'eo'), exhale, exit (cf. 'eo'), exude

ego, mei

pronoun

I, me

(N.B. 'me' is a good example of an accusative in English)

'alter ego' (cf. 'alter'), ego, egocentric, egoist, egomania, egotism, 'vade-mecum' (cf. 'cum')

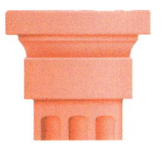 

E

egredior, egredi, egressus sum

verb *(third/fourth) (deponent)*

go out

egress, egresssion, egressive

emo, emere, emi, emptus

verb *(third)*

buy

'caveat emptor', emption

eo, ire, i(v)i

verb *(irreg.)*

go

circuit (cf. 'circum'), 'exeat', exit (cf. 'e, ex')

epistula, epistulae (fem.)

noun (1st)

letter

epistle, epistolarian, epistoler, epistolet, epistolography

A Latin Lexicon

equus

equus, equi (masc.)

noun (2nd)

horse

equestrian, equine

exercitus, exercitus (masc.)

noun (4th)

army

exercisable, exercise, exercitation

exspecto, exspectare, exspectavi, exspectatus

verb *(first)*

wait for, expect

expect, expectably, expectancy, expectation, expected

F

facilis, facile
adjective
easy
facile, facilitate, facilitation, facilitator, facilities

facio, facere, feci, factus
verb *(third/fourth)*
make, do
artefact (cf. 'ars'), benefactor (cf. 'bene'), fact, faction, factitious, factor, factory, factual

faveo, favere, favi, fautus (+ dative)
verb *(second)*
favour, support
favour, favourable, favoured, favourite, favouritism

A Latin Lexicon

felix, (gen.) felicis
adjective

fortunate, happy

felicitate, felicitations, feliciter, felicitous, Felicity, Felix

femina, feminae (fem.)
noun (1st)

woman

feminal, feminine, femininity, feminise, feminism

fero, ferre, tuli, latus
verb *(irreg.)*

bring, carry, bear

'confer' or 'cf.', feretory, relate, relationship, relative, transfer (cf. 'trans')

F

ferox, (gen.) ferocis
adjective
fierce, ferocious
ferocious, ferociousness, ferocity

festino, festinare, festinavi
verb *(first)*
hurry
festinate, festinately, festination

fidelis, fidele
adjective
faithful, loyal
fidelity, infidelity, 'semper fidelis' (cf. 'semper')

filius, filii (masc.)
noun (2nd)
son
affiliate, affiliation, filial, filially

A Latin Lexicon

flumen

flumen, fluminis (neut.)

noun (3rd)

river

flume

forte

adverb

by chance

fortuitous, fortuitously, fortuitousness, fortuity, fortune

fortis, forte

adjective

brave, strong

fortifiable, fortification, fortified, fortifier, fortify, fortifying

F

forum, fori (neut.)

noun (2nd)

forum, marketplace

forum

frater, fratris (masc.)

noun (3rd)

brother

fraternal, fraternisation, fraternise, fraternity, fratricide
(cf. 'mater', 'pater' and 'soror')

frustra

adverb

in vain

frustrate, frustrated, frustrating, frustratingly, frustration

fugio, fugere, fugi

verb *(third/fourth)*

run away, flee

fugitive, fugitively, fugitiveness, refuge, refugee (cf. 're')

G

gaudeo, gaudere, gavisus sum

verb *(second) (semi-deponent)*

be pleased, rejoice

gaud, gaudery, gaudiness, gaudy, gaudy-day/night
(cf. gaudium)

gaudeo

gaudium, gaudii (neut.)

noun (2nd)

joy, pleasure

gaud, gaudery, gaudiness, gaudy, gaudy-day/night
(cf. gaudeo)

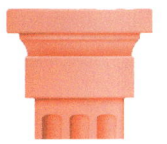 

G

gens, gentis (fem.)
noun (3rd)

family, tribe, race, people

genitive, gentile, gentilic, gentilism, gentilitian

gero, gerere, gessi, gestus
verb *(third)*

wear (clothes), wage (war)

belligerent (cf. 'bellum'), gestate, gestation, gestational, gestative

gladius, gladii (masc.)
noun (2nd)

sword

gladiate, gladiator, gladiatorial, gladiatorship, gladiolus

gravis, grave
adjective

heavy, serious

grave, gravimeter, gravitas, gravitate, gravitational, gravity

H

habito, habitare, habitavi, habitatus
verb *(first)*
live (in), inhabit, dwell
habit, habitat, habitation, habitual, habitudinal, inhabitable

hodie
adverb
today
hodiernal

homo, hominis (masc.)
noun (3rd)
man, human being
'homo sapiens', human, humane, humanist, humanitarian, humanity

H

hora, horae (fem.)
noun (1st)

hour

horologe, horologer, horologist, horology, horometry, horoscope

hortor, hortari, hortatus sum
verb *(first) (deponent)*

encourage, urge

exhort, exhortation, hortation, hortative, hortatory

hortus

hortus, horti (masc.)
noun (2nd)

garden

horticultural, horticulturalist, horticulture

A Latin Lexicon

hostis, hostis (masc.)

noun (3rd)

enemy

hostile, hostilely, hostilities, hostility

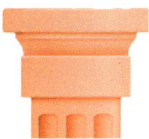 

I

N.B. 'i' becomes 'j' in many derivatives as the letter 'j' did not exist in the Roman alphabet; so 'Iulius Caesar' becomes Julius Caesar.

iaceo, iacere, iacui

verb *(second)*

lie (down)

adjacent, jacent

iacio, iacere, ieci, iactus

verb *(third/fourth)*

throw

adjective (cf. 'ad'), ejaculation, eject (cf. 'e, ex'), interject (cf. 'inter'), jaculator, object, projection (cf. 'pro'), subject (cf. 'sub')

ianua, ianuae (fem.)

noun (1st)

door

janitor, janitorial, janitorship, janitress, janitrix

A Latin Lexicon

ibi

adverb

there

'ibidem' or 'ib.' or 'ibid.' (cf. 'idem')

idem, eadem, idem

adjective/pronoun

the same

*'ibidem' or 'ib.' or 'ibid.' (cf. 'ibi'), 'idem' or 'id',
idempotency, idempotent (cf. 'possum'),
'semper idem' (cf. 'semper')*

imperator, imperatoris (masc.)

noun (3rd)

emperor; general, leader, commander

*empire, imperial, imperialism, imperialist, imperialistic, imperious
(cf. 'imperium and 'impero')*

imperium, imperii (neut.)

noun (2nd)

empire, power, command

*empire, imperial, imperialism, imperialist, imperialistic, imperious
(cf. 'imperator' and 'impero')*

I

impero, imperare, imperavi, imperatus (+ dative)

verb *(first)*

order, command

empire, imperial, imperialism, imperialist, imperiality, imperious
(cf. 'imperium and 'imperator')

in (+ ablative)

(also used as a prefix with verbs)

preposition

in, on

in, and as a prefix to many words, e.g. inception (cf. 'capio'), incite, include
(cf. 'in (+ accusative)')

in (+ accusative)

(also used as a prefix with verbs)

preposition

into, onto

into, and as a prefix to many words, e.g. incorporate, incubate, invade
(cf. 'in (+ ablative)')

A Latin Lexicon

incendo, incendere, incendi, incensus
verb *(third)*

burn, set on fire

incendiary, incendivity, incense (verb and noun), incensed

infelix, (gen.) infelicis
adjective

unlucky, unhappy

infelicitous, infelicity

ingredior, ingredi, ingressus sum
verb *(third/fourth) (deponent)*

enter

ingredient, ingress, ingression, ingressive

inimicus, inimici (masc.)
noun *(2nd)*

enemy

inimical, inimicality, inimically, inimicalness, inimicitous

I

insula

insula, insulae (fem.)

noun (1st)

island; block of flats

*insular, insularism, insulate, insulation, insulator,
peninsula, peninsular (cf. 'paene')*

intellego, intellegere, intellexi, intellectus

verb *(third)*

understand, realise

intellect, intellectual, intelligence, intelligent, intelligible

A Latin Lexicon

inter (+ accusative)

preposition

among, between

'inter alia' (cf. 'alius'), interact, intercept (cf. 'capio'), intercom, interim, interlude, interrupt (cf. 'interea')

interea

adverb

meanwhile

vide 'inter'

intro, intrare, intravi, intratus

verb *(first)*

enter, go in

enter, entering, entrance, entrant

invenio, invenire, inveni, inventus

verb *(fourth)*

find

invent, invention, inventive, inventiveness, inventory

I

invito, invitare, invitavi, invitatus
verb *(first)*

invite

invitation, invite, invitee, inviting, invitingness

ipse, ipsa, ipsum
pronoun

himself, herself, itself, *pl.* themselves

ipselateral, 'ipso facto'

ira, irae (fem.)
noun (1st)

anger

iracundity, irascibility, irascibly, irateness, ire
(cf. 'iratus')

iratus, irata, iratum
adjective

angry

iracundulous, irascible, irate, irately, ire, irefulness
(cf. 'ira')

A Latin Lexicon

is, ea, id
pronoun

he, she, it, *pl.* they; that, *pl.* those

'id est' or 'i.e.'

iter, itineris (neut.)
noun (3rd)

journey

itineracy, itinerant, itinerantly, itinerary, itinerate

iterum
adverb

again

iterance, iterate, iterative, reiterate (cf. 're-'), reiteration

I

iubeo, iubere, iussi, iussus

verb *(second)*

order

jussive

iuvenis, iuvenis (masc.)

noun (3rd)

young man

juvenile, juvenilely, juvenileness, juvenilise, juvenility

L

labor, laboris (masc.)

noun (3rd)

work, toil

laborious, labour, labourer, labourism, labourist
(cf. 'laboro')

laboro, laborare, laboravi

verb *(first)*

work, toil

laboriously, laboriousness, labour, laboured, laboursome
(cf. 'labor')

lacrimo, lacrimare, lacrimavi

verb *(first)*

weep, cry

lacrimal, lacrimary, lacrimation, lacrimose, lacrimosity

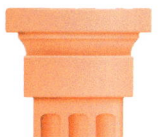

L

laetus, laeta, laetum
adjective
happy
laetare, Letitia

laudo, laudare, laudavi, laudatus
verb *(first)*
praise
applaud, applause, laud, laudable, laudatory

legio, legionis (fem.)
noun (3rd)
legion
legion, legionary, legionnaire

A Latin Lexicon

lego

lego, legere, legi, lectus

verb *(third)*

read; choose

elect, election, elective, lector, lecture, lecturer, re-elect (cf. 're')

lentus, lenta, lentum

adjective

slow, soft

relent, relenting, relentless, relentlessly

liber, libri (masc.)

noun (2ⁿᵈ)

book

librarian, librarianship, library

L

libero, liberare, liberavi, liberatus
verb *(first)*

free, set free

deliver, deliverance, liberate, liberation, libertarian, liberty
(cf. 'libertus')

libertus, liberti (masc.)
noun (2nd)

freedman, ex-slave

libertarianism, liberticide, libertinage, libertine, libertinism, liberty
(cf. 'libero')

locus, loci (masc. and neut.)
noun (2nd)

place

local, locality, location, locum, locus

longus, longa, longum
adjective

long

long, longevity, longing, longitude, longwise

A Latin Lexicon

loquor, loqui, locutus sum
verb *(third) (deponent)*

speak, talk

elocution, eloquent, loquacious, loquacity, magniloquent (cf. 'magnus'), pauciloquent (cf. 'pauci')

lux, lucis (fem.)
noun (3rd)

light, daylight

elucidate, lucency, lucid, lucidity, Lucinda, luxmeter, noctilucent (cf. 'nox'), translucent (cf. 'trans')

M

magnus, magna, magnum
adjective
big, large, great
magnificence, magnificent, magnifier, magnify, magniloquent (cf. 'loquor'), magnitude, Magnus

maior, maius
adjective (comparative of 'magnus')
bigger, greater
major, majority, majorly, majorship

malus, mala, malum
adjective
evil, bad
maleficent, malice, malign, malnourish, malpractice

A Latin Lexicon

maneo, manere, mansi
verb *(second)*

remain, stay

manse, mansion, mansionary, remain, remainder

manus, manus (fem.)
noun (4th)

hand; group of people

manual, manually, manufacture, manufacturer (cf. 'facio'), manuscript (cf. 'scribo')

mare

mare, maris (neut.)
noun (3rd)

sea

Marina, marina, marine, mariner, marines, maritime, submarine (cf. 'sub')

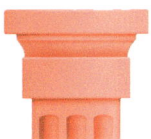

M

maritus, mariti (masc.)
noun (2ⁿᵈ)

husband

marital, maritally

mater, matris (fem.)
noun (3ʳᵈ)

mother

'alma mater', maternal, maternalism, maternalistic, maternally, maternity
(cf. 'frater', 'pater' and 'soror')

maxime
adverb

very greatly

vide **'maximus'**

maximus, maxima, maximum
adjective (superlative of 'magnus')

biggest, greatest, very big, very great

maximal, maximalist, Maximilian, maximise, maximum, Maxine

A Latin Lexicon

medius, media, medium
adjective

middle (of)

media, medial, median, mediation, Mediterranean (cf. 'terra'), medium

melior, melius
adjective (comparative of 'bonus')

better

ameliorate, meliorate, melioration, melioristic, meliority

meus, mea, meum
adjective/pronoun

my

'mea culpa'

miles, militis (masc.)
noun (3rd)

soldier

militant, militarise, military, militia

M

mille, pl. milia

number

1,000

millennium (cf. 'annus'), millennial, millimetre, millipede (cf. 'pes'), millisecond

minime

adverb

very little, least; no

vide 'minimus'

minimus, minima, minimum

adjective (superlative of 'parvus')

very little, smallest

miniature (mini-), minibus, minim, minimalist, minimise, minimum

minor, minus

adjective (comparative of 'parvus')

smaller, less

minor, minority, minus, minuscule, minutiae

A Latin Lexicon

miror, mirari, miratus sum
verb *(first) (deponent)*

wonder at, admire

admirably, admiration, miracle, miraculous, mirage, Miranda

miser, misera, miserum
adjective

miserable, wretched, sad

miser, miserable, miserably, miserly, misery

mitto, mittere, misi, missus
verb *(third)*

send

permit (cf. 'per'), premise, remiss, remit, remittance, remitting

modus, modi (masc.)
noun (2nd)

manner, way, kind

modal, mode, modish, module, 'modus operandi'

M

moneo, monere, monui, monitus
verb (second)
warn, advise
admonish, admonishment, monition, monitor, monitory

mons, montis (masc.)
noun (3rd)
mountain
mount, mountain, mountaineering, mountainous, mounted

morior, mori, mortuus sum
verb (third/fourth) (deponent)
die
immortal, immortalise, immortality, mortal, mortality
(cf. 'mors')

mors, mortis (fem.)
noun (3rd)
death
mortalise, mortally, mortuary, post-mortem (cf. 'post')
(cf. 'morior')

A Latin Lexicon

moveo, movere, movi, motus

verb *(second)*

move

movable, move, movement, movie, moving

multo

adverb

much, by much

vide 'multus'

multus, multa, multum

adjective

much, *pl.* many

multi-, multicultural, multimedia, multilinguist, multiple, multiplication, multitude

M

murus, muri (masc.)

noun (2nd)

wall

mural, muralist, muriform

N

narro, narrare, narravi, narratus
verb *(first)*

tell, relate

narratable, narrate, narration, narrative, narrator

nauta, nautae (masc.)
noun (1st)

sailor

aquanautics (cf. 'aqua'), nautical, nautically, nautics

navigo, navigare, navigavi
verb *(first)*

sail

circumnavigate (cf. 'circum'), navigability, navigable, navigate, navigation, navigational
(cf. 'navis')

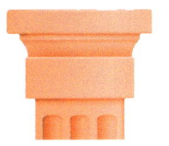 

N

navis, navis (fem.)

noun (3rd)

ship

navaid, naval, navalism, navy
(cf. 'navigo')

nescio, nescire, nescivi

verb *(fourth)*

not know

nescience, nescient
(cf. 'scio')

nihil (neut.)

noun/pronoun *(irreg.)*

nothing

annihilate, annihilation, nihilism, nihilist, nil, nilpotent (cf. 'possum')

nolo, nolle, nolui

verb *(irreg.)*

not want, refuse

nolition
(cf. 'volo')

A Latin Lexicon

nomen, nominis (neut.)

noun (3rd)

name

denomination, nomenclature, nominal, nominative, nominee, noun

non

adverb

not

non-, e.g. non-drip, non-executive, non-mover, non-profitmaking, nonsense

nos, nostrum

pronoun

we, us

'inter nos', nostrum

novem

number

nine

November, novenary, novennial (cf. 'annus')

N

novus, nova, novum
adjective

new

novate, novation, novel, novice, renovation

nox

nox, noctis (fem.)
noun (3rd)

night

noctambulation, noctambulist, (cf. 'ambulo'), noctilucent (cf. 'lux'), noctivagant, nocturnal, nocturne

nullus, nulla, nullum
adjective

not any, no…

null, nullification, nullifidian, nullify, nullity

A Latin Lexicon

nuntio, nuntiare, nuntiavi, nuntiatus

verb *(first)*

announce, report

announce, announcement, announcer, renounce, renounceable, renouncement
(cf. 'nuntius')

nuntius, nuntii (masc.)

noun (2nd)

messenger, message, news

announce, announcement, announcer, renounceable, renouncement, renouncer
(cf. 'nuntio')

O

octo
number
eight
oct-, octagon, octave, October, octopus, octuplet

offero, offerre, obtuli, oblatus
verb *(irreg.)*
offer
oblate, offer, offeree, offering, offeror, offertory, proffer (cf. 'pro')

omnis, omne
adjective
all, every
omnibenevolent (cf. 'bene'), omnibus, omnificent (cf. 'facio'), omnipotent (cf. 'possum'), omnipresent (cf. 'sum'), omniscient (cf. 'scio'), omnivore

A Latin Lexicon

opprimo, opprimere, oppressi, oppressus

verb *(third)*

crush, overwhelm

oppress, oppression, oppressive, oppressiveness, oppressor

oppugno, oppugnare, oppugnavi, oppugnatus

verb *(first)*

attack

oppugn, oppugnancy, oppugnant, oppugner
(cf. 'pugno')

optimus, optima, optimum

adjective (superlative of 'bonus')

best, excellent, very good

optimal, optimise, optimism, optimist, optimistic, optimum

O

oro

oro, orare, oravi, oratus

verb *(first)*

beg

orate, oration, orator, oratorial, oratory

ostendo, ostendere, ostendi, ostentus

verb *(third)*

show

ostensible, ostensibly, ostensive, ostentation, ostentatious

P

paene

adverb

almost, nearly

peninsula, peninsular, peninsularity (cf. 'insula'), penult, penultimate, penumbra

paro, parare, paravi, paratus

verb *(first)*

prepare, provide

preparation, preparative, preparatory, prepare, prepared, 'semper paratus' (cf. 'semper')

pars, partis (fem.)

noun (3rd)

part

part, partial, participle, particle, parting, partition

P

parvus, parva, parvum
adjective

small

parvanimity, parvovirus

pater, patris (masc.)
noun (3rd)

father

*paternal, paternalism, paternalistic, paternally, paternity
(cf. 'frater', 'mater' and 'soror')*

patior, pati, passus sum
verb *(third) (deponent)*

suffer, endure

impassive, passion, passionate, passive, patience, patient

patria, patriae (fem.)
noun (1st)

country, homeland, fatherland

Patricia, Patrick, patriot, patriotic, patriotism, repatriate

A Latin Lexicon

pauci, paucae, pauca
adjective (pl.)

few, a few

pauciloquent (cf. 'loquor'), paucity

pax, pacis (fem.)
noun (3rd)

peace

pacifiable, pacifier, pacifism, pacifist, pacify

pecunia, pecuniae (fem.)
noun (1st)

money

impecunious, pecuniarily, pecuniary, pecunious

peior, peius
adjective (comparative of 'malus')

worse

pejorate, pejoration, pejorative, pejoratively (cf. note under 'I')

P

pello, pellere, pepuli, pulsus
verb *(third)*

drive

expel, expulsion, impulsive, pulsate, pulse, repel

per (+ accusative)
preposition

through, along

perceive, 'per centum' or 'per cent' (cf. 'centum'), percussion, permeate, permission, permit (cf. 'mitto'), perturb (cf. 'turba')

pereo, perire, perii
verb *(irreg.)*

die, perish

perish, perishability, perishable, perished, perishing

periculum, periculi (neut.)
noun (2nd)

danger

peril, perilous, perilously, perilousness

A Latin Lexicon

persuadeo, persuadere, persuasi (+ dative)

verb *(second)*

persuade

persuadable, persuade, persuader, persuasion, persuasive, persuasiveness

perterritus, perterrita, perterritum

adjective

terrified

terrified, terrify, terrifying, terrifyingly, terror, terrorism (cf. 'terreo')

pes

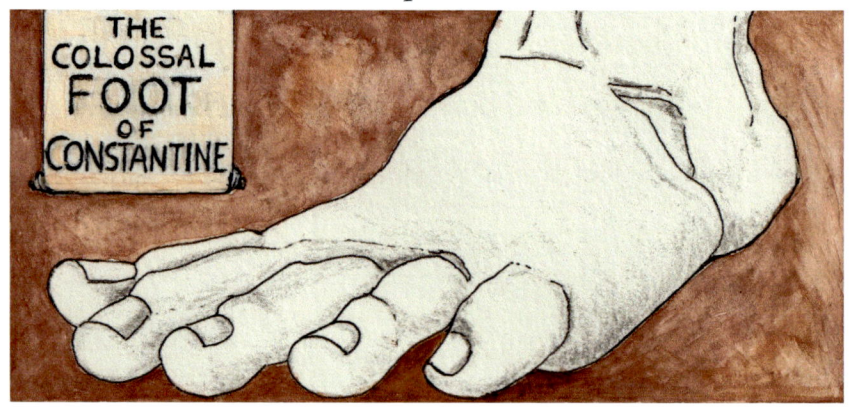

pes, pedis (masc.)

noun (3rd)

foot

centipede (cf. 'centum'), millipede (cf. 'mille'), pedal, pedestrian, pedicab, pedicure (cf. 'cura'), pedometer

 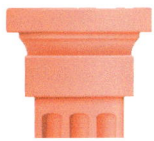

P

pessimus, pessima, pessimum
adjective (superlative of 'malus')

worst, very bad

pessimal, pessimism, pessimist, pessimistic, pessimum

peto, petere, petivi, petitus
verb *(third)*

make for, seek, beg for, ask for, attack

compete, competent, competition, petition, petitioner, petitioning

plurimus, plurima, plurimum
adjective (superlative of 'multus')

very much, *pl.* very many, most

vide 'plus'

plus, (gen.) pluris
adjective (comparative of 'multus')

more of (+ gen.); *pl.* more

plural, pluralism, pluri-, e.g. pluripresence (cf. 'sum'), plus

A Latin Lexicon

poena, poenae (fem.)

noun (1ˢᵗ)

punishment

penal, penalisation, penalise, penally, penalty

pono, ponere, posui, positus

verb *(third)*

put, place, set up, put up

deposit, deposition, pose, posit, positioning, postpone (cf. 'post'), preposition, transpose (cf. 'trans')

porta, portae (fem.)

noun (1ˢᵗ)

gate

port, portal

porto, portare, portavi, portatus

verb *(first)*

carry, bear, take

deport, deportation, portability, portable, porter, portfolio, transport (cf. 'trans')

P

possum, posse, potui
verb *(irreg.)*

can, be able

*idempotent (cf. 'idem'), impossible, nilpotent (cf. 'nihil'),
omnipotent (cf. 'omnis'), possibility, possible*

post (+ accusative)
preposition

after, behind

*postdate, postdoctoral, 'post meridiem' or 'p.m.' (cf. 'dies'),
post-mortem (cf. 'mors'), postpone (cf. 'pono'),
'post scriptum' or 'P.S.' (cf. scribo)*

postea
adverb

afterwards

vide 'post'

praemium, praemii (neut.)
noun (2nd)

prize, reward, profit

premium

A Latin Lexicon

primo
adverb

at first

vide 'primus'

primus, prima, primum
adjective

first

'prima facie', primary, primate, prime, primitive, primordial

princeps, principis (masc.)
noun (3rd)

chief; emperor

prince, princedom, principal, principality, principle

pro (+ ablative)
preposition

in front of, for, in return for

proactive (cf. 'ago'), 'pros and cons' (cf. 'contra'), proffer (cf. 'offero'), pro-forma, 'pro rata', 'quid pro quo' (cf. 'quis?')

P

procedo, procedere, processi
verb *(third)*

advance, proceed

procedure, proceed, process, procession, processionary, processor

proficiscor, proficisci, profectus sum
verb *(third) (deponent)*

set out

profectitious

progredior, progredi, progressus sum
verb *(third) (deponent)*

advance

progress (verb and noun), progression, progressionary, progressionist, progressive

promitto, promittere, promisi, promissus
verb *(third)*

promise

promise, promisee, promising, promisor, promissive, promissory

A Latin Lexicon

proximus, proxima, proximum
adjective

nearest, next to

approximate, approximation, proximal, proximate, proximity

puer, pueri (masc.)
noun (2nd)

boy

puerile, puerilism, puerility

pugno, pugnare, pugnavi
verb (first)

fight

*pugnacious, pugnaciousness, pugnaciousnessly, pugnacity
(cf. 'oppugno')*

pulcher, pulchra, pulchrum
adjective

beautiful, handsome

pulchritude, pulchritudinous

P

punio, punire, punivi, punitus

verb *(fourth)*

punish

punish, punishable, punisher, punishment, punition, punitive

puto, putare, putavi, putatus

verb *(first)*

think

putative, putatively

Q

quaero, quaerere, quaesivi, quaesitus
verb *(third)*
search for, look for, ask
enquiry, inquiry, query, quest, question, questionnaire

quaero

qualis?, quale?
adjective
what sort of?
quale, qualified, qualify, qualitative, quality

Q

quantus? quanta? quantum?
adjective
how big? how much?
quantifiable, quantify, quantitative, quantity, quantum

quattuor
number
four
quadrangle, quadrilateral, quadruple, quarter, quartet, quatercentenary (cf. 'centum'), quaternary, quaternate

qui, quae, quod
pronoun
who, which
'quod erat demonstrandum' or 'Q.E.D.', 'quod vide' or 'q.v.', quorate, quorum, 'status quo'

A Latin Lexicon

quinque
number

five

quincentenary (cf. 'centum'), quinqu(e)-, quinquefoliate, quinquennial (cf. 'annus'), quintuplet

quis?, quid?
pronoun

who?, what?

'quid pro quo' (cf. 'pro'), quiddity, 'quidnunc'

quot?
adjective

how many?

quota, quotation, quote, quotidian (cf. 'dies'), quotient

R

rapio, rapere, rapui, raptus
verb *(third/fourth)*

seize, grab

enrapture, rapacious, rapacity, rape, rapture

re- (a prefix used with verbs)
prefix

…back

reconvene (cf. 're' and 'convenio'), recur (cf. 'curro'), re-elect (cf. 'lego'), refugee (cf. 'fugio'), regain, reinstate, reiterate (cf. 'iterum'), renounce, repeat, return

refero, referre, rettuli, relatus
verb *(irreg.)*

bring back, carry back; report, tell

refer, referee, referral, relate, related, relation, relative

A Latin Lexicon

regina, reginae (fem.)

noun (1st)

queen

regal, regally, regency, regent, Regina/Gina, regius
(cf. 'regnum', 'rego' and 'rex')

regnum, regni (neut.)

noun (2nd)

kingdom

regal, regalian, regality, regency, regnal, regnant
(cf. 'regina', 'rego' and 'rex')

rego, regere, rexi, rectus

verb *(third)*

rule, reign

regent, regentship, regiment, regimental, regular, regulate
(cf. 'regina', 'regnum' and 'rex')

regredior, regredi, regressus sum

verb *(third/fourth) (deponent)*

go back, return

regress, regression, regressive, regressivity

R

relinquo, relinquere, reliqui, relictus
verb *(third)*

leave, leave behind

relic, relict, relinquish, relinquished, relinquishment, reliquary

res, rei (fem.)
noun (5th)

thing, matter, event, business

're'

resisto, resistere, restiti (+ dative)
verb *(third)*

resist

irresistible, resist, resistance, resistible, resistivity, resistor

respondeo, respondere, respondi, responsus
verb *(second)*

reply

irresponsible, respond, responder, response, responsible, responsive

A Latin Lexicon

rex, regis (masc.)

noun (3rd)

king

*regalia, regalist, regally, regius, Rex
(cf. 'regina', 'regnum' and 'rego')*

rideo

rideo, ridere, risi

verb *(second)*

laugh, smile

deride, derision, derisory, rident, ridicule, ridiculous

rogo, rogare, rogavi, rogatus

verb *(first)*

ask, ask for

rogation, rogatory

S

sacer, sacra, sacrum
adjective
sacred
sacrament, sacred, sacrifice, sacrificial, sacrilege

saluto, salutare, salutavi, salutatus
verb *(first)*
greet
salutary, salutation, salutational, salute, saluter

sanguis, sanguinis (masc.)
noun (3rd)
blood
sanguiferous, sanguify, sanguine, sanguinely, sanguivorous

 *A Latin Lexicon*

scelestus, scelesta, scelestum

adjective

wicked

scelerate
(cf. 'scelus')

scelus, sceleris (neut.)

noun (3rd)

crime

scelerate
(cf. 'scelestus')

scio, scire, scivi, scitus

verb *(fourth)*

know

nescient (cf. 'nescio'), omniscient (cf. 'omnis'), science, scient, scientific, scientist

scribo, scribere, scripsi, scriptus

verb *(third)*

write

manuscript (cf. 'manus'), 'post scriptum' or 'P.S.' (cf. 'post'), scribble, scribe, script, scripture

S

sedeo, sedere, sedi
verb *(second)*

sit

sedent, sedentarily, sedentariness, sedentary

semper
adverb

always

*'semper fidelis' (cf. 'fidelis'), 'semper idem' (cf. 'idem'),
'semper paratus' (cf. 'paro'), sempervivum (cf. 'vivo'), sempiternal*

senator, senatoris (masc.)
noun (3rd)

senator

senate, senate-house, senator, senatorial, senatorship

senex, senis (masc.)
noun (3rd)

old man

senile, senilely, senility, senior, seniority

A Latin Lexicon

sentio, sentire, sensi, sensus
verb *(fourth)*

feel, notice

sense, senseless, sensory, sensual, sentence, sentiment

septem
number

seven

September, septennial (cf. annus), septuplet

sequor, sequi, secutus sum
verb *(third) (deponent)*

follow

consequence, second, sequacious, sequel, sequence, sequential

servo, servare, servavi, servatus
verb *(first)*

save, keep, protect

conservation, conservatory, conserve, observe, preserve, reserve

S

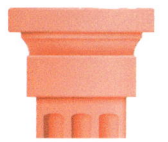 

servus, servi (masc.)

noun *(second)*

slave[2]

servile, servility, servitude

sex

number

six

sex-, sexcentenary, sexennial (cf. annus), sexpartite, sextuplet

sic

adverb

thus, in this way

'sic', 'sic passim'

---

[2] Avoid translating 'servus' as servant.

A Latin Lexicon

silva

silva, silvae (fem.)

noun (1ˢᵗ)

wood

silva, silvan, silvatic, silvestrian, siviculture

simul

adverb

at the same time

simultaneity, simultaneous, simultaneously, simultaneousness

sine (+ ablative)

preposition

without

sinecure (cf. 'cura'), 'sine die', 'sine dubio', 'sine qua non'

S

soleo, solere, solitus sum
verb *(second) (semi-deponent)*

be accustomed

insolence, insolent, obsolescence, obsolescent, obsolete

solus, sola, solum
adjective

alone, lonely, only, on one's own

solitary, solitude, solitudinarian, solivagant, solo

soror, sororis (fem.)³
noun (3ʳᵈ)

sister

sororal, sororial, sorority
(cf. 'frater', 'mater' and 'pater')

specto, spectare, spectavi, spectatus
verb *(first)*

look at, watch

spectacle, spectacled, spectacular, spectate, spectator, spectatorship

---

[3] 'soror' is not included in the OCR List but it seemed unbalanced to omit the 'sorority' when mothers, fathers and brothers appear; and the derivatives for all four family members provide useful comparisons for each other.

A Latin Lexicon

spero, sperare, speravi, speratus

verb *(first)*

hope, expect

despair, desperate, desperation
(cf. 'spes')

spes, spei (fem.)

noun *(fifth)*

hope

despair, desperate, desperation
(cf. 'spero')

sto, stare, steti

verb *(first)*

stand

stance, standing, station, stationary, stationery, 'stet'

stultus, stulta, stultum

adjective

stupid, foolish

stultification, stultified, stultifier, stultify, stultifying

S

sub (+ accusative/ablative)
preposition
under, beneath
submarine (cf. 'mare'), submerge, subordinate, subsidiary, substandard, suburban (cf. 'urbs'), subway

subito
adverb
suddenly
subitaneous, subitise

sum, esse, fui
verb *(irreg.)*
be
essence, essential, essentialism, 'id est' or 'i.e.', presence, present

summus, summa, summum
adjective
highest, greatest, top (of)
sum, 'summa cum laude' (cf. 'cum' and 'laudo'), summit, summitless

A Latin Lexicon

supero, superare, superavi, superatus

verb *(first)*

overcome, overpower

insuperable, superable, superably, superate, superation

surgo, surgere, surrexi

verb *(third)*

get up, stand up, rise

resurge, resurgence, surge, surgeful, surgent, surging

T

taberna, tabernae (fem.)
noun (1st)
shop, inn
tabernacle, tabernacular, tavern, taverna, taverner

taceo, tacere, tacui, tacitus
verb *(second)*
be silent, be quiet, keep quiet
tacit, tacitly, tacitness, taciturn, taciturnity, taciturnly

talis, tale
adjective
such, of such a kind
talesman
(N.B. different from talisman)

A Latin Lexicon

tandem

tandem
adverb
at last, finally
(in) tandem, tandem

tempestas, tempestatis (fem.)
noun (3ʳᵈ)
storm
tempest, tempestive, tempestuous, tempestuously, tempestuousness

templum, templi (neut.)
noun (2ⁿᵈ)
temple
templar, temple, templed

T

tempus, temporis (neut.)

noun (3rd)

time

contemporaneous, contemporary, 'pro tempore' or 'pro tem.' (cf. 'pro'), temporal, temporary, temporise, tense

teneo, tenere, tenui, tentus

verb *(second)*

hold

abstain (cf. 'ab'), tenable, tenacious, tenacity, tenancy, tenure

terra, terrae (fem.)

noun (1st)

ground, land, country, earth

extraterrestrial, Mediterranean (cf. 'medius'), 'terra firma', terrace, terracing, terrene, terrestrial

terreo, terrere, terrui, territus

verb *(second)*

frighten

terrified, terrify, terrifying, terrifyingly, terror, terrorism (cf. 'perterritus')

A Latin Lexicon

timeo, timere, timui
verb *(second)*
fear, be afraid
timid, timidity, timidly, timidness, timorous

tollo, tollere, sustuli, sublatus
verb *(third)*
raise, lift up, hold up
sublate, sublation

tot
adjective
so many
tot (up) (cf. 'totus')

totus, tota, totum
adjective
whole
total, totalise, totalitarian, totality, totally

T

trado, tradere, tradidi, traditus
verb *(third)*

hand over, hand down

tradition, traditional, traditionalist, traditionalistic, traditionally

traho, trahere, traxi, tractus
verb *(third)*

drag

protractor, retract, retractable, tract, tractable, traction, tractor

trans (+ accusative)
(also used as a prefix with verbs)

preposition

across

transatlantic, transcend, transfer (cf. 'fero'), translation, translucent (cf. 'lux'), transport (cf. 'porto'), transpose (cf. 'pono'), transvestite

tres, tria
number

three

tri-, triad, triangle, triathlon, triceps (cf. 'caput')

A Latin Lexicon

tristis, triste

adjective

sad

triste, tristesse

turba, turbae (fem.)

noun (1ˢᵗ)

crowd

perturb, perturbance (cf. 'per'), turbid, turbulator, turbulence, turbulent

U

ubi

adverb

where, when, with '?' = where?

ubiety, ubiquarian, ubiquitary, ubiquitous, ubiquity

unus, una, unum

number

one

uni-, unicorn, uniform, unify, unitard, unity, universe (cf. 'verto'), university

urbs, urbis (fem.)

noun (3rd)

city, town

suburban (cf. 'sub'), urban, urbane, urbanism, urbanite

uxor

uxor, uxoris (fem.)

noun (3ʳᵈ)

wife

uxorial, uxorially, uxorilocal (cf. 'locus'), uxorious

V

validus, valida, validum

adjective

strong

invalid, invalidate, valid, validate, validation, validity

vehementer

adverb

violently, loudly

vehemence, vehemency, vehement, vehemently

vendo, vendere, vendidi, venditus

verb *(third)*

sell

vend, vendibility, vendible, vending, vendition, vendor

 *A Latin Lexicon*

venio, venire, veni

verb *(fourth)*

come

advent (cf. 'advenio'), circumvent (cf. 'circum'), contravene (cf. 'contra'), convenient, convent, convention, reconvene (cf. 're' and 'convenio')

verbum, verbi (neut.)

noun (2nd)

word

adverb (cf. 'ad'), cruciverbalist, verb, verbal, verbality, verbatim, verbose

verto, vertere, verti, versus

verb *(third)*

turn

convert, divert, reverse (cf. 're'), verse, version, vertebra, 'vice versa'

via, viae (fem.)

noun (1st)

street, road, way

via, viaduct (cf. 'duco')

V

victoria, victoriae (fem.)

noun (1ˢᵗ)

victory

Victor, victor, Victoria, victorious, victoriousness, victory
(cf. 'vinco')

video, videre, vidi, visus

verb *(second)*

see

audio-visual (cf. 'audio'), video, visa, visibility, vision, vista, visual

villa, villae (fem.)

noun (1ˢᵗ)

house, country villa

villa, village

vinco, vincere, vici, victus

verb *(third)*

conquer, win, be victorious

vanquish, vanquishable, vanquisher, Vincent
(cf. 'victoria')

A Latin Lexicon

vinum

vinum, vini (neut.)

noun (2ⁿᵈ)

wine

vine, vinegar, vineyard, viniculture, vintage, vintner

vir, viri (masc.)

noun (2ⁿᵈ)

man, male

virago, virile, virilescence, virility, virtue
(cf. 'virtus')

V

virtus, virtutis (fem.)
noun (3rd)
courage, virtue
virtual, virtue, virtuosity, virtuous, virtuously
(cf. 'vir')

vita, vitae (fem.)
noun (1st)
life
'curriculum vitae' or 'C.V.', Vita, vital, vitality, vitamin

vivo, vivere, vixi
verb *(third)*
live, be alive
sempervivum (cf. 'semper'), vivacious, vivacity,
'viva voce' or 'viva' (cf. 'vox'), Vivian, vivid, vividness, vivisection

voco, vocare, vocavi, vocatus
verb *(first)*
call
vocabulary, vocal, vocalise, vocation, vocative
(cf. 'vox')

A Latin Lexicon

volo, velle, volui

verb *(irreg.)*

want, wish, be willing

benevolent (cf. 'bene'), volition, volitive, voluntarily, voluntary, volunteer (cf. 'nolo')

vox, vocis (fem.)

noun (3rd)

voice, shout

*'viva voce' or 'viva' (cf. 'vivo'),
vocal, vocals, vocative, vociferate, vociferous (cf. 'voco')*

vulnero, vulnerare, vulneravi, vulneratus

verb *(first)*

wound, injure

invulnerable, vulnerability, vulnerable, vulnerary, vulnerate, vulneration (cf. 'vulnus')

vulnus, vulneris (neut.)

noun (3rd)

wound

invulnerable, vulnerability, vulnerable, vulnerary, vulnerate, vulneration (cf. 'vulnero')

FINIS